Canadian Holidays

Victoria Day

Jill Foran

Weigl

CALGARY

Published by Weigl Educational Publishers Limited
6325 – 10 Street SE
Calgary, Alberta, Canada
T2H 2Z9
Web site: www.weigl.com

National Library of Canada Cataloguing in Publication Data
Foran, Jill
        Victoria Day

(Canadian holidays)
Includes index.
ISBN 1-894705-98-X

        1. Victoria Day--Juvenile literature. I. Title. II. Series: Canadian holidays (Calgary, Alta.)
GT4813.A2F595 2002   j394.262'0971   C2002-900818-2

We acknowledge the financial support of the Government of Canada through the Book Publishing
Industry Development Program (BPIDP) for our publishing activities.

Printed in the United States of America
1 2 3 4 5 6 7 8 9 0 06 05 04 03 02

Project Coordinator Heather Kissock **Design** Warren Clark
Copy Editor Jennifer Nault **Layout** Bryan Pezzi **Photo Researcher** Nicole Bezic King

Photo Credits

Every reasonable effort has been made to trace ownership and to obtain permission to reprint copyright material. The
publishers would be pleased to have any errors or omisssions brought to their attention so that they may be corrected in
subsequent printings.

Cover: The Royal Collection ©2002, Her Majesty Queen Elizabeth II; **Barrett & Mackay Photography Inc:** page 10; **Cecil
Beaton/CAMERA PRESS/PONOPRESSE:** page 15M; **Burnaby Village Museum:** page 18L; **www.canadianheritage.org
ID# 20474, Ontario Archives OA457:** page 9L; **Cheadle Photography Inc.:** page 11T; **Corel Corporation:** pages 3,
19R, 19T; **Courtesy Department of Canadian Heritage:** page 14; **DigitalVision:** page 17L; **Glenbow Archives:** pages 8
(NA-2878-64), 9R (ND-3-3233), 13L (NA-3965-15); **Tim Graham/CORBIS/MAGMA:** pages 5R, 12; **Lyn Hancock:** page 18R;
Robin Karpan: page 18M; **Heather Kissock:** pages 20, 21; **Clarence W. Norris/Lone Pine Photo:** pages 11B, 17R, 22;
National Archives of Canada: pages 4 (C-008133), 7B (C-052232), 15B (C-9945), 16R (C-113827); **Skjold Photography:**
15T; **Jim Steinhart of www. PlanetWare.com (http://www.PlanetWare.com):** pages 5L, 7T; **Upper Canada Village/c/o
The St. Lawrence Parks Commission:** page 19B; **Veterans Affairs Canada:** page 13R; **Marilyn "Angel" Wynn:** page 16L.

Contents

Introduction

This holiday honours the birth of Queen Victoria.

Victoria Day is celebrated each year on the Monday before May 25. This national holiday honours the birthday of Queen Victoria, the ruling **monarch** of the British **Empire** from 1837 to 1901. On Victoria Day, Canadians also honour the birth of today's **reigning** monarch, Queen Elizabeth II. To many Canadians, Victoria Day signals the beginning of summer. Many spend the Victoria Day weekend opening their summer cottages. Others head to Canada's national parks for hikes, picnics, and other outdoor activities.

Victoria was only 18 years old when she became queen.

Victoria Day is a uniquely Canadian holiday. No other country, not even England, still observes Queen Victoria's birthday as an official holiday. Also, no other country honours the birthday of Queen Elizabeth II in May. By honouring these two queens, Canada is paying tribute to its British **heritage**. It is also showing its continued loyalty to the British monarchy.

In the 1950s, it was established that Canadians would celebrate Queen Elizabeth II's birthday on Victoria Day. Queen Elizabeth's real birthday is on April 21. In England, her birthday is celebrated in June.

Buckingham Palace, in London, England, is the queen's official residence.

The Origins of Victoria Day

Victoria's reign was a prosperous era in British history.

Queen Victoria was one of the most respected rulers in British history. Born on May 24, 1819, Victoria became queen of the United Kingdom of Great Britain and Ireland when her uncle, William IV, died in 1837. Victoria's reign was a **prosperous** era in British history. During her reign, Great Britain took control of India. It was also during this time that some of Britain's **colonies**, such as Canada and Australia, united to become countries. All of these changes brought power and wealth to Great Britain. During this period, the British Empire was at its peak. Queen Victoria became a symbol of the empire's strength. Her reign lasted 63 years, which is the longest reign of any British monarch.

Victoria's empire stretched to all parts of the world.

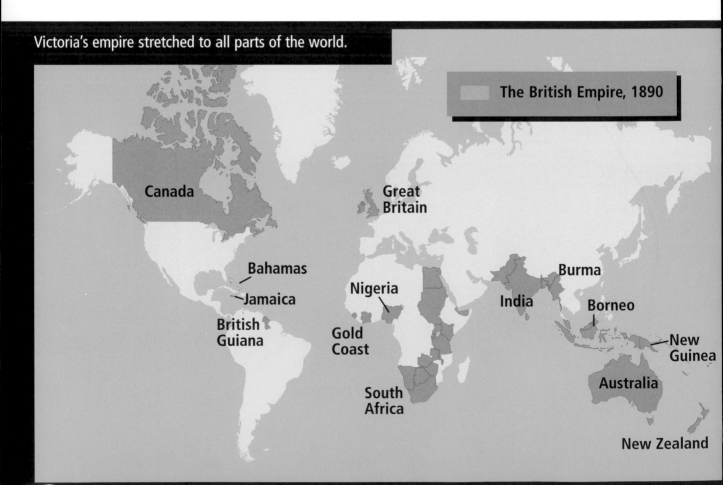

The British Empire, 1890

Canada

Great Britain

Bahamas

Jamaica

British Guiana

Nigeria

Gold Coast

South Africa

India

Burma

Borneo

New Guinea

Australia

New Zealand

Canadians have been celebrating Victoria Day for more than 150 years. The tradition began in 1845, when the people of **Canada West** declared Queen Victoria's birthday, May 24, an official holiday. By making May 24 an official holiday, the people of Canada West were showing their loyalty to the queen and her empire. After Canada became a country in 1867, Canadians continued to celebrate the queen's birthday as a sign of loyalty.

Empire Day

In the late 1890s, a woman from Hamilton, Ontario brought special meaning to the queen's birthday. Clementina Fessenden thought it would be a good idea to honour both the British Empire and Canada's British heritage on a certain day every year. It was decided that this holiday should be celebrated on a date close to Queen Victoria's birthday. The day chosen was the last school day before May 24. The day was called Empire Day. It was first celebrated in Canada in 1897. When Queen Victoria died in 1901, the Canadian government decided to blend Empire Day and the queen's birthday into one official holiday called Victoria Day.

Queen Victoria married Prince Albert in 1840.

An Old-Fashioned Victoria Day

Children performed plays about Canada and the British Empire.

Canadians have always regarded Queen Victoria's birthday as a time for festivity. In the late 1800s and early 1900s, people throughout the country celebrated Queen Victoria's birthday on May 24. However, if May 24 fell on a Sunday, Victoria Day was moved to May 25. By doing this, the Victoria Day celebrations did not interrupt Sunday church services.

Much like today, many people celebrated Victoria Day with large family picnics.

Early Victoria Day celebrations in Canada were filled with fun activities and special tributes to the British Empire. In towns and cities across Canada, church bells were sounded, cannons were fired, marching bands performed in parades, and fireworks displays lit up the night sky. Children often staged plays or pageants about Canada and the British Empire. Many Canadians also took part in a traditional British game called **cricket**.

Although she took great interest in her Canadian subjects, Queen Victoria never once set foot in Canada.

Many Canadian cities and towns, including Toronto, held parades to celebrate Queen Victoria and the British Empire.

Brought to Canada 150 years ago by the British army, cricket was once a very popular sport.

Canadians celebrate Victoria Day with fun activities.

In 1952, the Canadian government stated that the celebration of Victoria Day would take place on the Monday before May 25. This decision meant that there would always be a long weekend at the end of May. Today, Canadians continue to celebrate the Victoria Day weekend with fun activities. Many host picnics and large parties, while others participate in special sporting events and tournaments. Throughout the day, people set off firecrackers. At night, fireworks light up the sky.

Parties with friends and family are a favourite way to celebrate Victoria Day and the coming summer.

The Victoria Day weekend also marks the beginning of the summer season for many Canadians. In most parts of Canada, the snow has melted, and the leaves are budding by the time this long weekend arrives. People look forward to Victoria Day as a time to enjoy the outdoors. Thousands of Canadians go camping or hiking, while others plant their gardens.

Victoria Day in Victoria

Victoria Day celebrations have special meaning in Victoria, British Columbia, a city that was named after the queen. Every year, Victoria holds a special ten-day festival that begins on the Victoria Day weekend. The Victoria Harbour Festival features a number of fun events that pay tribute to Queen Victoria and the British Empire. These events include a Victorian costume contest, a display of **vintage** British cars, and a huge family picnic at Beacon Hill Park. The city also hosts an enormous parade on this day. Thousands of people gather to see colourful floats, decorated cars, and costumed citizens. More than forty marching bands also make their way along Victoria's downtown streets.

Campgrounds throughout the country are very busy during the Victoria Day long weekend.

A Royal Anthem

This song pays tribute to the monarch.

Canada's royal **anthem** is called "God Save the Queen." For more than 100 years, Canadians have sung this special song to pay tribute to the monarch and the rest of the Royal Family. It is believed that "God Save the Queen" was written in England in the 1600s. It was first heard in public in 1745, following a British battle. Over the centuries, it has been sung as an expression of loyalty to the British monarchy.

Queen Elizabeth and her husband, Prince Philip, first visited Canada in 1951. The family has come to Canada many times since then, for tours and important Canadian ceremonies.

God Save the Queen

God save our gracious Queen
Long live our noble Queen,
God save the Queen:
Send her victorious,
Happy and glorious,
Long to reign over us:
God save the Queen.

O lord, our God, arise,
Scatter thine enemies,
And make them fall:
Confound their politics,
Frustrate their knavish tricks,
On thee our hopes we fix:
God save us all.

Thy choicest gifts in store,
On her be pleased to pour,
Long may she reign:
May she defend our laws,
And ever give us cause
To sing with heart and voice
God save the Queen.

Until the late 1900s, children across Canada would sing "God Save the Queen" at the beginning of each school day. Today, Canadians still sing this royal anthem on occasions that honour the queen and her family. In some parts of Canada, it is sung at special Victoria Day ceremonies. It is also played for members of the Royal Family whenever they visit Canada.

In Canada, Queen Victoria has had more places and buildings named for her than any other person in history.

Queen Elizabeth II's parents, King George VI and Queen Elizabeth, spent 6 weeks travelling across Canada in a royal train in 1939. Crowds greeted them wherever they went.

Prince Charles, Queen Elizabeth II's oldest child, has visited Canada fifteen times.

Royal Symbols in Canada

Canada displays many royal symbols.

All across Canada, cities and towns display symbols that represent the country's ties to British royalty. This Victoria Day, try to spot some of these symbols:

The Arms of Canada

One of the country's most respected emblems is a banner known as the Arms of Canada. It shows a shield surrounded by several symbols that represent parts of Canada's history and culture. Many of the symbols found on the Arms of Canada show the country's link to the British monarchy. One of the most important royal symbols is the **Imperial** Crown, which sits atop the Arms of Canada. The crown represents the presence of a monarch as Canada's **head of state**.

The Royal Union Flag

The Royal Union flag is more commonly known as the "Union Jack." It is the national flag of the United Kingdom. It also has a long history in Canada. The Union Jack was one of Canada's national symbols in the early 1900s. Today, the flag is often displayed in Canada as a symbol of loyalty to Great Britain. On holidays such as Victoria Day, the Union Jack is flown at **federal** buildings, airports, military bases, and other buildings in Canada.

The Great Seal of Canada

A seal is a sticker or stamp that is attached to a document. The Great Seal of Canada is used on all of the country's official documents. The seal shows the monarch dressed in robes, sitting on the **coronation** chair, and holding an **orb** and a **sceptre**. The Great Seal of Canada reminds Canadians that the British monarch is Canada's head of state.

A Day to Celebrate

Victoria Day is also known as Bread and Cheese Day.

Some Canadians celebrate different holidays on the Victoria Day weekend. On the Six Nations Reserve near Brantford, Ontario, Victoria Day is known as Bread and Cheese Day. Every year on this day, people who live on the reserve gather at their community centre to receive gifts of bread and cheese. This tradition first began on May 24, 1837, when Queen Victoria thanked Canada's Native Peoples for being Great Britain's **allies** in many battles. At first, blankets were given as gifts. In later years, the gifts were bread and cheese. Today, the reserve also includes outdoor games and cultural displays in its Bread and Cheese Day celebrations.

Lacrosse is a game that was first played by Native Peoples in Eastern Canada. It is now Canada's national sport.

War Chief Joseph Brant helped the British fight many battles.

Canadians living in Québec also celebrate a different holiday on Victoria Day. They celebrate *Fête de Dollard des Ormeaux*. This holiday honours a soldier who fought for **New France** in the 1600s. French Canadians throughout Québec celebrate this day with games, picnics, and other special activities.

Some Canadians refer to Victoria Day as "Firecracker Day" because it is one of the most popular holidays for setting off fireworks and firecrackers.

Spending time with friends is a great way to enjoy the holiday.

Many families enjoy good weather and time off in local parks.

Canadians Celebrate!

Here are just some of the ways that people across Canada celebrate Victoria Day:

In Burnaby, British Columbia, many people attend the Victoria Day celebration at the Burnaby Village Museum. This celebration features old-fashioned carousel rides, children's crafts, farm activities, and **Maypole** dancing in a large meadow. In the afternoon, everyone takes part in a toast to the Queen, and then enjoys a slice of delicious birthday cake.

In Regina, Saskatchewan, thousands of people go to Wascana Park to celebrate Victoria Day. They enjoy large picnics with their family and friends, live music, and fun outdoor games.

Cambridge Bay

In Cambridge Bay, Nunavut, the May long weekend marks the beginning of a ten-day festival called Omingmak Frolics. Events at the festival include snowmobile racing, ice sculpting, and traditional Arctic games.

Burnaby

Regina

In New Ross, Nova Scotia, many people spend Victoria Day planting pumpkins at the official Pumpkin Planting Party on Ross Farm.

In St. John's and other parts of Newfoundland, many people celebrate the Victoria Day weekend by taking part in large trout expeditions. This tradition began in 1900 with the Trouters' Special.

Just east of Morrisburg, Ontario, the Upper Canada Village hosts an old-fashioned Victoria Day celebration. Visitors to the village take part in events similar to those that

took place on Victoria Day in the 1860s. They sing "God Save the Queen," listen to historical speeches, watch military demonstrations, and take part in traditional Victorian games.

St. John's

New Ross

Morrisburg

Fun Things to Do

One of the most popular outdoor pastimes on Victoria Day is going on a picnic. To make your Victoria Day picnic special, here are some fun things to prepare:

Cucumber Sandwiches

Materials needed:
- 225 mL softened cream cheese
- 25 mL half-and-half cream
- 25 mL snipped fresh chives
- 1 loaf or 12 slices of rye or wheat bread
- 1 English (seedless) cucumber, cut into thin slices
- 24 fresh basil leaves
- 1 round cutter

Instructions:
In a bowl, beat together the cream cheese and cream until the mixture is smooth and soft. Stir in the chives. With a round cutter, stamp out two rounds from each slice of bread. Spread the cream cheese mixture on the rounds of bread, then top them with several slices of cucumber and basil.

Tea Scones

Materials needed:
- 500 mL flour
- 12 mL baking powder
- 25 mL sugar
- 2 mL salt
- 75 mL butter
- 125 mL buttermilk
- 1 lightly beaten egg
- 1 biscuit cutter

Instructions:
Mix dry ingredients. Add 12 mL of butter and mix until the mixture is crumbly. Pour in the buttermilk. Mix until the dough is sticky and clings together. On a lightly floured surface, roll out the dough until it is 2 cm thick. With a biscuit cutter, stamp the dough into rounds. Transfer the rounds to a cookie sheet and brush them with the lightly beaten egg. Bake at 220° C for 15 minutes, or until light brown. Serve with jams and jellies.

A Victoria Day Quiz

1 **True or False?** Canada is the only country that celebrates the birthday of Queen Elizabeth II in May.

2 **When was Queen Victoria's actual birthday?**
a. April 21
b. May 24
c. May 25
d. July 1

3 Which holiday do most people in Québec celebrate instead of Victoria Day?

a. Empire Day
b. Bread and Cheese Day
c. fête de Dollard des Ormeaux
d. May Day

5 True or False?
Canada has always celebrated Victoria Day on the Monday before May 25.

4 Who was responsible for creating Empire Day in 1897?

a. Clementina Fessenden
b. Queen Victoria
c. Dollard des Ormeaux
d. Queen Elizabeth II

6 True or False?
Queen Victoria's reign lasted 75 years.

Answers 1. True 2. b 3. c 4. a 5. False In the late 1800s and early 1900s, Victoria Day was celebrated on May 24 or May 25. 6. False. Queen Victoria reigned for 63 years.

Words to Know

allies: helpers

anthem: a song of praise

Canada West: present-day Ontario

colonies: territories ruled by another country

coronation: the crowning of a monarch

cricket: an outdoor game that is popular in England

Empire: a group of countries run by one government or ruler

federal: concerning the central government of Canada

head of state: the official head of a country

heritage: something that has been handed down from the past; a tradition

Imperial: representing an empire

Maypole: a pole decorated with ribbons and flowers around which people dance

monarch: a king or a queen

New France: a historical part of Canada that is now called Québec

orb: a sphere or globe

prosperous: having success, wealth, or good fortune

reigning: ruling

sceptre: a royal wand or rod

vintage: classic, old-fashioned

Index